TWENTY-ONE DAYS

By Forrest Jamison

Twenty-One Days

Trilogy Christian Publishers A Wholly Owned Subsidiary of Trinity Broadcasting Network

2442 Michelle Drive Tustin, CA 92780

Copyright © 2022 by Forrest Jamison

Rights Department, 2442 Michelle Drive, Tustin, CA 92780.

Trilogy Christian Publishing/TBN and colophon are trademarks of Trinity Broadcasting Network.

Cover design by: Lauren Gomez

For information about special discounts for bulk purchases, please contact Trilogy Christian Publishing.

Trilogy Disclaimer: The views and content expressed in this book are those of the author(s) and may not necessarily reflect the views and doctrine of Trilogy Christian Publishing or the Trinity Broadcasting Network.

Manufactured in the United States of America

10 9 8 7 6 5 4 3 2 1

Library of Congress Cataloging-in-Publication Data is available.
ISBN: 978-1-68556-729-3
E-ISBN: 978-1-68556-730-9

Table of Contents

Introduction

Purpose. I'm sure we are all very familiar with the word "purpose." I know this all too well. I have used it many times when asking myself, "What is my purpose?" Some of us go through life with no purpose; we simply live life. Some are confident in their purpose, while others are always looking *for* a purpose. While I was growing up, I lived as if there was no purpose.

In 2009, I changed that by taking my walk with Jesus seriously and, consequently, began struggling with discovering my own life's purpose.

A few years ago, I realized that the root of my struggle lay deeper; it was with the core meaning of the word "purpose" itself, which is "the meaning of life." When we ask God and ourselves, "What is my purpose in this life?" what we are truly asking is, "What is the *meaning* of my life?"

We all have the innate desire to matter and make a difference in this world, but how can we do that if we don't know our purpose?

While reading the Parable of the Sower in Mark, chapter 4, I questioned the purpose of parables. Two purposes come to mind:

1. To help us understand the heart of God.
2. To help us understand how things work in the kingdom of God.

The true meaning of life is described in the Parable of the Sower. According to the parable, our purpose in life is to cultivate a heart that is receptive to hearing and accepting the redemptive message of Jesus' death and resurrection and to live a life that produces a bountiful harvest that can spiritually feed a multitude.

I have realized over the years that our lives are intended to be a source of life-giving nutrition for everyone around us, and the only way we can produce that kind of fruit is to provide good soil for the seeds that God wants to plant in us. The meaning of life, according to Jesus, is to do whatever it takes to continuously offer Him fertile soil, to give ourselves to understanding Him and His kingdom, to constantly deepen our souls by pursuing the truth about ourselves and God, and to set aside our worries and material ambitions so that we trust God above all.

What is the purpose of my life? What is the meaning of my life? Well, it is to help those around me to see God in everyday life through the experiences that He has pushed, pressed, and pulled me through.

As you read this book and you turn each page, I ask that you have an open heart and open mind to receive whatever God wants to teach you during the next twenty-one days.

Day One: Puzzle Pieces

On January 15, 2015, my wife and I sat together with my parents in the doctor's office of the cancer building as we waited to hear my dad's test results. The results: stage four lung cancer. As the doctor spoke with us about the procedures, I couldn't help but drift off and think about the things that I hadn't done and still wanted to do with my dad. Thoughts flooded my mind then, denial hit. I was silently praying, *God, is this it? There is more to this, isn't there?* When my mind returned to reality, the talk was over, and the doctor had left the room. I broke down.

I thought we had finished, so I left the waiting room and went out front. As I walked toward the exit, I saw a round table with an uncompleted puzzle laid out on the surface. It seemed awkward to me. I kept looking at it, focusing on the missing pieces. I even tried to put some together as my wife talked to her mom on the phone. As we went back into the waiting room, I wrote down, "Puzzle pieces." I knew right then that my view of life was about to change.

Have you ever realized how many similarities there are between puzzles and life? In a puzzle, each piece plays an important part in the big picture. In life, people and events play important parts. As with pieces of a puzzle, each of us is unique, special in our own way. Although we may appear similar, there are no two alike. Ironically, it is our differences that make us fit. While I was thinking about that puzzle, it occurred to me that there is always *that one piece* that we are certain belongs in *that particular spot*, but when we go to place it, it does not fit. Even though that piece doesn't fit, we keep going back to it, trying to *make* it fit, forgetting or ignoring the fact that we have already tried because we have our minds set on the idea that a particular piece belongs there.

Think about how often that has happened in your life; times you have tried to make things happen that just weren't meant to be. I'm sure we all have tried over and over again to make a piece of the puzzle fit, even to the point of forcing it into the empty space, but because that piece was not created for that place in the puzzle, there was nothing we could do to change it.

If you have ever put a puzzle together, you know what it is like to spend time looking for one specific piece. We think we know what it looks like, it seems so obvious, but we can't find it. We become so wrapped up in finding that one piece that we can't see beyond it. We grow so frustrated that we decide to let it go and step away from it for a while. When we come back to it, we end up finding the missing piece immediately because it was right in front of us all along.

Life has been like this for me at times. I try so hard to understand why things happen the way they do. I search high and low for the answers, and sometimes, the answers are right in front of me. It isn't until I stop and take a step back, breathe, and let it go, that I find the answers.

As I thought about the table with the puzzle, I thought about the pieces in my life; my family, my friends, events, milestones, and celebrations. There is such a mixture of good and bad, joy and tears, happiness and sorrow. I thought about all those pieces that I didn't feel were important or had a purpose. I reflected on all of the pieces in my life that have caused me to ask, "Why me, God? Why this?" I realized that the pieces I agonized over were the pieces of the puzzle that allowed all of the others to fall into place.

The cliché "everything happens for a reason" is so true, either due to our decisions or God's. Each event, whether good or bad, signifies a piece of the puzzle. If you take away one piece, it upsets the harmony of the finished product. I finally understand that even though some of the pieces in my life aren't pleasant and many of them bring me pain and heartache, without them, I couldn't move on. No matter how unimportant I think they are, they bring me one step closer to wholeness.

We can't possibly look at the pieces of our lives at any given moment and understand the important role that each one of them plays; there are too many holes, and the picture isn't clear. However, I know when my journey in this life comes to an end and that final piece is put into place, I'm going to look back and understand. I will no longer wonder why there was so much pain, why certain people came and went, or why certain events transpired in my life. I will be able to see the beauty of the complete picture and the perfection of the pieces of the plan that made it whole.

Until then, I will continue to live on faith, knowing and trusting that the pieces I need are there and that it will only be a matter of time before they fall into place. I will remember that there is a bigger picture that I'm unable to see at present and that, as Jeremiah 29:11 says, "He knows the plans that He has for me." I will believe that each piece of my life, even the painful ones, has a purpose and play an important role. When I'm weak, I will seek strength through prayer.

I do all this in the hope that on that glorious day, He will whisper to me, "Well done."

~Amen.

Today, reflect on the pieces of your life and how they fit together or don't fit together. Be grateful for the pieces in your life, good or bad.

Day Two: The Battle

While en route to Papua New Guinea, I was sitting in the Dallas Fort Worth Airport in the Admiral Club Lounge. I had just finished reading a book called *The Shack*.

The book made me think about all sorts of things as I read it. There is one particular part in the story where a man is headed to the shack. He was afraid to go because he did not know what he would find when he arrived, but he had to go through with it. The book described the man getting out of his truck in the snow-covered woods and walking toward the shack. The man took one step forward, and then one step back, then one step forward, and again, one step back. As I read that scene, it occurred to me how afraid the man was to do what he had no choice but to do. As frightened as he was, he had to keep pressing on.

Have you ever felt that way? I have been in that place many times throughout my life. At times, I've felt like the only way to walk the path was with my eyes closed, praying it would all work out. I can recall a few times in my journey when God had called me to do something when I double and triple-checked to make sure He really wanted me to do it. Then, with courage and faith, I took that first step through the door that God was knocking on. Through these experiences, I have learned that the beauty in this life is that we belong to Him. We are vessels that He is using, even though we are cracked, broken, chipped, and even shattered. God has chosen *us* to be vessels for Him.

The reality is, when we give up and live for Christ, it isn't always going to be easy. Life is going to bring daily challenges. It is how we choose to trust God and react and deal with those challenges that will determine whether things go smoothly or horribly. As the Psalms tell us, we are equipped with strength for the battle, and victory is ours. We really need to believe it. "For You have armed me with strength for the battle; You have subdued under me those who rose up against me" (Psalm 18:39, NKJV).

~Amen.

Today, reflect on a struggle or battle that you are experiencing. Ask yourself, "Am I worried whether I would be able to conquer my battle?" Understand that whatever battle or mountain you are climbing, God's Word states we "are armed with strength for the battle."

Day Three: Green Light Special

"Whoever is patient has great understanding, but one who is quick-tempered displays folly" (Proverbs 14:29, NIV).

Allow me to paint a picture for you. You're pressed for time and stuck at a stoplight waiting for the light to turn green. You start muttering under your breath, "Come on already!" With a hard sigh, you continue, "Just turn green!"

Don't laugh. We've all been there. The longer you wait, the more likely you are to start asking questions like, "Why are you taking so long!? What is the deal!?" As if the inanimate object directing the flow of traffic will give you an answer. Most of us have expressed similar queries to drivers of vehicles ahead of us in traffic, even though we know they can't hear what we say. We've all witnessed some interesting hand gestures in traffic as well.

There is some realism and hard-to-swallow truth in this example. Don't we treat God that way at times? We do it when we pray for something that we desire, such as a car, an answer to financial difficulty, a family, a better job, or just simple guidance. The list goes on and on. The reality is, the longer we wait, the more frustrated we become. When we feel frustrated, we start asking, "God, why aren't you answering me? Why is it taking so long? Why must I always be patient with You?" We ask these questions even though we know in the back of our minds that it will happen when the time is right, or so we hope. We all experience these thoughts and emotions in our walk with God and want that "green light."

I have been through this before; in fact, I have been part of both scenarios. I have been the person yelling at the stoplight and at the driver in front of me in traffic, who could not hear me. I have been the person wondering where God was and why I hadn't received an answer to prayer. The truth of the matter is God never left. He had answered me, but I had been too wound up in my emotions and the "have to have it now" mindset to see or hear the answer.

Have you ever wondered why patience matters so much? I know when I was a child, I had to use it to get things I wanted. In adulthood, patience has come to mean something more profound. The question is, why does patience matter so much?

Second Peter 3:9 (NIV) states, "The Lord is not slow in keeping his promise, as some understand slowness. Instead, he is patient with you, not wanting anyone to perish, but everyone to come to repentance."

This verse gives us the answer. God Himself is patient, so why shouldn't we be patient? God's timing is perfect. Waiting for God is tougher than taking matters into our own hands. Sometimes, you will wait hours, months, or even years, for what you are praying for. When that prayer is answered, all is well. The reason why the wait was so long, or why the answer wasn't given immediately, becomes clear. We need to be patient for that "green light" and not give in to impatience so we don't miss out on the blessings in store for us.

~Amen.

Today, reflect on being patient with others, yourself, and most importantly, with God. Remember to be patient with the faults of others if you expect them to have patience with yours.

Day Four: Forgotten Promises

While in Papua New Guinea, I had just finished with my day and decided to go for a run along the runway in Kiunga. As I was running, I was listening to the song "Nothing Is Wasted" by Elevation Worship. As I listened to this song, I felt God's presence and looked up at the sky and saw this view of the sky.

As I looked at this view, it reminded me of how beautiful and peaceful Papua New Guinea is and how awesome my God is. It reminded me that I don't have a boring God; no, I have a *wow* God! I was also reminded of Jacob and how he knew God was with him wherever he traveled. That brought me to the account of Jacob's life in Genesis 28:10–19.

There are a lot of details in Jacob's story. I will try not to bore you, but God met me there in that story and helped me see things that I had forgotten or had not yet seen.

Jacob was running from something in his life. We need to understand from this example that God shows up in the many struggles we face and reveals Himself in ways we might not otherwise notice at other times in our lives. In Genesis 28:13, God reminds Jacob of the promises He has for him. I believe there are promises that God has spoken over my life and yours we have allowed the world to get in front of. Perhaps, as you read further, you too will remember the forgotten promises God has for your life.

In Genesis 28:14, we encounter one of the biggest reminders: that we are not here merely to enjoy the comfort and presence of God, but that we also need to go into the world and take the blessing of God and share it with those around us.

For me, the story gets real in Genesis 28:19. It says, "He called that place Bethel, though the city used to be called Luz." Isn't it interesting how one encounter with God can rename a situation in our lives?

Sometimes, we forget that God is all around us. I believe God is waking us up on the inside and opening our eyes to see His glory in all things. God is with us through our trials. God is with us during our lonely seasons. God is with us in our dry places. I have come to learn that I don't just feel and see God's presence. I carry His presence wherever I go in life.

My prayer is that God will open our eyes to see His glory in every situation and keep us awake throughout this journey we call life.

~Amen.

Today, reflect on the promises God has for you and your family. Remember that you are blessed to be a blessing to those around you.

Day Five: Worries

So, there I was, sitting in an airplane that I had been minutes away from missing, saying to myself, *I was so worried that I wasn't going make this flight. My wife was worried but told me that I would make it.* That situation made me stop to reflect on how frequently I worry about things that I don't even need to be worried about.

I started thumbing through my notes because I remembered reading an article about a study on worry and anxiety. I read that the average human spends almost an hour of every waking day feeling worried and anxious. The study illustrated what the average person's worries and anxiety are focused on. The results were as follows.

Forty percent: Things that will never happen.

Thirty percent: About the past that can't be changed.

Twelve percent: About criticism by others (mostly untrue).

Ten percent: About health, which gets worse with stress.

Eight percent: About real problems that will be faced.

Here is what Jesus says, "But seek first the kingdom of God and His righteousness, and all these things shall be added to you. Therefore, do not worry about tomorrow, for tomorrow will worry about its own things. Sufficient for the day is its own trouble" (Matthew 6:33–34, NKJV).

Based on these numbers, we spend nearly an hour a day worrying needlessly. To me, this seems like a miserable existence, but I am just as guilty of this as everyone else. Think about this, we worry all the time. Ironically, when we worry all the time, we start to think about how often we worry. Then, we begin to worry that we worry too much. Does that sound familiar? It is a never-ending cycle, and there is only one way to break it. We have to stay focused on the task at hand, stay focused on our purpose in life and on what we are here on earth for. The only way to find that is to fill our minds with scripture and prayer through a relationship with Jesus.

In the book of Luke, Jesus tells His disciples, "Therefore I say to you, do not worry about your life, what you will eat; nor about the body, what you will put on" (Luke 12:22, NKJV).

Focus on the part where Jesus said, "*Do not worry* about your life." That is big, it's huge! However, it's not easy. We all have reasons to worry. There are times that it seems impossible not to worry about situations in our lives or even in the lives of others. So, where can we turn for a hopeful or helpful word? There is nothing and no one better than Jesus. He knows the future and every detail of our lives.

In 1 Peter 5:6–7 (NKJV), we are told, "Therefore humble yourselves under the mighty hand of God, that He may exalt you in due time, casting all your care upon Him, for He cares for you."

Jesus wants us to understand that we don't gain anything in our lives by *worrying*. Instead, worrying distracts us from the One who knows what we need and when we need it. We are called to trust in Him, knowing that our Lord will meet our needs in His good time.

I'm learning day by day that our tomorrows are too easy to take for granted. One day, our tomorrow will be gone. It's important to live for Christ today. What does it mean to live for Christ? I know I struggle with that question from time to time, but as I walk through this journey called life, I have come to believe it's turning to Him for help and showing His love to others. It's trusting He will provide just enough for today.

~Amen.

Today, reflect on today. A lot of us are fighting tomorrow's battles with today's strength. We need to stop wasting today's strength fighting tomorrow's battles.

The narrow truth is, every day has its problems, troubles, and sorrows, but because of who we are in Christ, it will truly be alright.

Day Six: Time and Boundaries

The God who made the world and everything in it is the Lord of heaven and earth and does not live in temples built by human hands. And He is not served by human hands, as if He needed anything. Rather, He gives everyone life and breath and everything else. From one man He made all the nations, that they should inhabit the whole earth; and He marked out their appointed times in history and the boundaries of their lands. God did this so that they would seek Him and perhaps reach out for Him and find Him, though He is not far from any one of us.

Acts 17:24–27 (NKJV)

While I was reading Acts, this section stood out boldly to me. I kept reading it repeatedly until God revealed something to me. Look at the part where it says, "Appointed times and boundaries." Do you know what that means? I sure didn't; God had to spell it out for me. After I researched the definitions, it finally hit me that it says that God has "determined the times" set for us and the "exact places" where we would be and live.

That brought me to Proverbs 20:24: "Man's steps are ordained by the Lord. How then can man understand His way?" We may not understand our path, but God has been guiding our every step. It is not a mistake that we are where we are. God has positioned us here. Despite all the wrongs and pain we have been through, we have been intentionally placed in positions in order for God to use us for a greater good. I have come to believe that that *greater good* could be any of these four things:

- To draw us into a relationship with Him.
- To develop our character and make us more like Him.
- To show us how He can overcome any obstacle.
- To reveal His glory.

I have learned that all of us walk a unique path, but we sometimes limit how far we walk along that path by giving in to doubt, fear, and feelings of inadequacy. God's calling for each of us is like a fingerprint. Therefore, we need to keep our focus on His divine path for us and keep walking patiently down our unique paths and know Jesus is with us.

It says in the Word, "Therefore we also since we are surrounded by so great a cloud of witnesses, let us lay aside every weight and the sin which so easily ensnares us, and let us run with endurance the race that is set before us…" (Hebrews 12:1)

The truth is, if we were to know everything that God knows, we would not have had or want it any other way.

~Amen.

Today, reflect on where you are in your life. Ask God to help you appreciate where He has placed you and help you value others and love as He loves.

Day Seven: Endurance

Have you ever wondered what separates us from others in athletics, education, business, or any other endeavor we undertake during our lifetime? I believe it is our drive to do more than is expected or required of us. The saying "go the extra mile" comes to mind. This saying goes way back to the days of the Roman soldiers. The soldiers would place boulders out on the trails as mile markers. When they passed residents of the places they had conquered, the soldiers would demand that the locals carry the soldier's pack for a mile, and the locals had to comply. Imagine if just one of those locals went an extra mile without getting upset and did it out of the kindness of their heart.

Jesus spoke of going the "extra mile" in this verse, "…And whoever compels you to go one mile, go with him two…" (Matthew 5:41, NKJV)

I feel the second mile that Jesus is talking about is the secret to success in life. However, when we focus on this second mile, we tend to forget about the first mile. Jesus is speaking of going two miles or the "extra mile," but the first mile of hard work is required of us as well. We cannot just skip the first mile and end up on the second mile without first exerting the effort to arrive at that point.

I believe the Christian life has its own mandated mile that is motivated by God's Law. This first mile is always tough to start because it always interrupts our schedule when we start walking it. The first mile causes us to swallow our pride and bear an extra burden. Examples of this in everyday life include beginning an exercise program, dieting, helping others, scripture memorization, and anything else that requires discipline to enable us to take that first step. When I think about Matthew 5:41, I think we play leapfrog with it. What I mean is, we want to enjoy the perks of the second mile, but we do not want to deal with the requirements it takes to walk that first mile.

I call the second mile the "Miracle Mile." What this means is that this mile separates some individuals from others. The second mile is only made possible by being obedient to the first mile. The second mile has a way of brightening our own road. Those who journey on this "Miracle Mile" have a way of lightening the load of those around them. One cannot go the second mile without influencing others. However, it only takes one second miler in a home to change the entire environment. It only takes one second miler on a team or in the office to do the same. The "Miracle Mile," the second mile, is motivated by the *love of Christ*.

The second mile is the mile our Lord Himself walked. He knows this road all too well. It was love that took Him on the "Miracle Mile" to the cross. He journeyed the first mile; He stepped out of heaven and into human flesh. He walked the mandated first mile that was motivated by the law. He kept every detail of the law, but He also went the second mile. He was motivated by His own love for us. He who made the stars with a spoken word and formed the universe, the one who formed and fashioned us with His own hands, said, "I love you, and I will walk with you." But we went our own way, turning away from Him. Then He said, "I will go the second mile." That took Him to the cross, where He bore the weight of our sins.

The second mile is when blessings are poured down because we are doing more than what is required of us. There are times we ask ourselves, "What did I get myself into?" or "Why am I doing so much?"

I can tell you what I believe; I believe it's because this verse is embedded into our very core.

We are not all we ought to be today, but we can be much more, only if we choose to walk the first mile and then go the second.

~Amen.

Today, reflect on going the extra mile. Thank God for pushing you and giving you the grace to do more than what is required in life. Focus on how you can continue to push further so He will be glorified.

Day Eight: Wheel Concept

While running through the streets of a village called Kiunga, located in central Papua New Guinea, I happened to notice a local riding a bike. When I was on my way back, he was walking it. As I ran past him, I looked at the wheels on the bike. I could not stop thinking about those wheels. *Do you ever get the feeling that God is about to teach you something?* That day, He did.

Take a few moments to study a wheel from a bicycle or an old wagon. If you don't have either of those items handy, picture one in your mind's eye, or look one up on Google Images. When you study the wheel, you will notice a central hub that connects to the spokes that extend outward to the outer part of the wheel. Notice that if it weren't for the central hub, the wheel would not be stable. The center hub stabilizes and holds the wheel together.

There is an idea floating around that God, church, and other spiritual matters are spokes in the wheel of a person's busy life. At some point, we've all said, "I go to church," in much the same way we would say, "I go to the gym." Here is the truth of the matter;

the Word makes it perfectly clear that God's desire is not to have God as one spoke on the wheel of our lives but to have Him as the hub. Sometimes we sectionalize our spiritual life. Our job is in one section, our family in another, our spiritual life in another, and God in another. We sectionalize our lives in this manner while knowing that life works best when we bring God into the center of our lives, which, in turn, stabilizes all the rest. God can bring change, health, and growth to every aspect of our lives, from our jobs to our social lives and any other relationship and interest we have. If we care about it, God cares about it.

Make Him the hub from which everything else stems. If we do that, then the wheel of our life will be stabilized.

~Amen.

Today, reflect on the fact that all of God's creations have a reason to be joyful because of how great He is. Take a moment to consider every aspect of your life and ask yourself, "Does it all belong to God? Does it all reflect praise toward Him?" Our lives are just like a wheel with spokes. God is the central hub, and He should be part of the entire thing, not just a portion.

Day Nine: Obedience

"For we walk by faith, not by sight" (2 Corinthians 5:7).

Have you ever asked yourself what it means to "walk by faith, not by sight"? Have you ever wondered what 2 Corinthians 5:7 really means? Have you ever contemplated the meaning of faith? The 1828 Webster's Dictionary definition of faith is "…to *trust*, to *draw* towards anything, to *believe*, to *obey*."

The apostle Paul reminds us that followers of Jesus must build their lives around things that have eternal significance rather than pursuing the same things the world pursues. A Christian should focus on the unseen realities, such as Jesus and heaven. Paul goes on to say, "Therefore we make it our aim, whether present or absent, to be well-pleasing to Him. For we must all appear before the judgment seat of Christ, that each one may receive to what he has done, whether good or bad" (2 Corinthians 5:9–10).

Jesus wants us to know that walking by faith means living life in light of eternal consequences. To walk by faith is to fear God more than man; to *obey* the Bible even when it conflicts with man's commands; to choose righteousness over sin, no matter what the cost; to *trust* God in every circumstance; and to *believe* God rewards those who seek Him, regardless of who says otherwise (read Hebrews 11:6).

Rather than loving the things of this world, as it states in 1 John 2:15–16, we should spend our time glorifying God in everything we do (1 Corinthians 10:31). It requires faith to live this way because we cannot see, hear, or touch anything spiritual. When we base our lives on the truth of God's Word rather than on the popular horoscope of the day, we are going against our natural inclinations. Our natural instincts may be to horde money, but when we walk by faith, we are to give to those in need (Luke 11:41; Ephesians 4:28). Society may say that sexual immorality is acceptable, but those who walk by faith base their standards on the unchangeable nature of God's Word, which states that any sex outside of marriage is sin (1 Corinthians 6:18; Ephesians 5:3; Galatians 5:19). Walking by faith requires that we tune our hearts to the voice of the Holy Spirit and the truth of His Word (John 10:27; John 16:13).

The information about faith in scripture and how the verses intertwine with each other is amazing. Do you remember the story in Joshua, chapter 6? The story about how God spoke to Joshua about leading the Israelites into battle to conquer the great walls of Jericho? The theme of faith is woven throughout it. God said to Joshua:

> March around the city once with all the armed men. Do this for six days. Have seven priests carry trumpets of rams' horns in front of the ark. On the seventh day, march around the city seven times, with the priests blowing the trumpets. When you hear them sound a long blast on the trumpets, have the whole army give a loud shout; then the wall of the city will collapse and the army will go up, everyone straight in.
>
> Joshua 6:3–5

Joshua commanded the army, "Do not give a war cry, do not raise your voices, do not say a word until the day I tell you to shout. Then shout!" (Joshua 6:10).

You may be wondering what all that has to do with faith. Well, all of us have promises that we want to see fulfilled. We have dreams and desires that we want to see realized. Most of all, we want to see progress made in the pursuit of our promises and desires. I bet that the Israelites felt the same way while walking around a city for six days without seeing anything happen. You would think God would have given them a sign to motivate them, to let them know that what He promised them was really going to happen. Nope. God did nothing. Not a single brick fell from the walls of Jericho on the first day or even on the sixth day of marching around the city.

Have you ever felt like that? I know I have. I've felt like screaming to God, "Where is the sign? All I need is a sign that you are working here, that my faith is working here! When is it going to end? How much longer do I need to keep going?" I imagine the Israelites thought the same thing. I bet they even thought it was impossible to get into Jericho. Why do I say that? Because in Joshua 6:1, it states, "Now the gates of Jericho were securely barred because of the Israelites. No one went out, and no one came in." Do you ever feel like your promises are locked up, and you can't get through the gate to reach them? Do you ever feel like the end goal is impossible to achieve? What I have learned through experience is that impossible situations are not intimidating to God. He welcomes them.

Scripture says that Jericho barred up their walls because of the Israelites. You see, the people of Jericho had heard about God's people; they had heard about the great deeds that God had done for them; they had heard about the victories that God had won; how He brought them across the Jordan River; how He delivered them from the hands of Pharaoh. The people of Jericho were scared.

From this, we learn much of the fear we experience is just a sign that our enemy is afraid of us. It could be a sign that the enemy knows he cannot keep us out of those locked gates that bar us from God's promises any longer, that our seventh lap is almost here.

God says, "We are to walk by faith, not by sight." God is telling Joshua that he will have to walk around those walls and believe that He is working even though it does not seem to be working at all. They walked for six days without any visible results. Maybe we are on our second month or second year of walking around our own personal Jericho without visible results. Here is a life lesson; just because our progress isn't visible, it doesn't mean our faith isn't working. We have to learn to take another lap when nothing moves.

Again, we must walk by faith, not by sight. Sometimes God doesn't want us to see or know He is working because He wants to do a deep work in us. I bet that, on the seventh day when the Israelites took over the city of Jericho, there was more work done inside of them than we can fathom. I believe God also wants us, once we get inside our promise, to remember and glorify the One who brought us there.

~Amen.

Today, reflect on the promise that God is preparing for you. Don't stop praying, and don't stop seeking. Focus on today and wait for God to wave His white flag showing you this is your last lap.

Day Ten: Plans

I have had this scripture on my lock screen since the first day I moved back to Nebraska. It has been the light at my feet and the reality check of my movements. Despite the path we *feel* God is pointing us down and the path He is actually guiding us along, saying, "Go this way and follow me," we often go the other way. This scripture doesn't say *you* know the plans; it implies you *don't* know, but God knows the plans He has for you. Mary had a plan, and Joseph had a plan. God had other plans.

God wants us to make a plan for our lives, but that plan is always subject to change at His notice. The important thing to remember is that, while the plan may change, the promise still stands. He *still* promises you hope. He *still* promises you a future. He *still* promises you deliverance. He *still* promises you His love.

So, please don't hold so tightly to your plans that you miss His purpose. After all, if everything happened according to Joseph and Mary's plans, we wouldn't have Emmanuel.

~Amen.

Today, reflect on the plans that God wants to work through you. Remember, God has plans to give you hope and a future.

Day Eleven: Directions

People who are searching for something want clear directions. Some people don't think it matters how you seek God or what you believe about Him. The world's definition is not helpful to people who truly want a relationship with God. God's Word, on the other hand, gives very clear instructions. It does not treat all beliefs as equal. Instead, it points to the only path, which is through Jesus. In Matthew 7:13–14, He states, "Enter through the narrow gate. For wide is the gate, and broad is the road that leads to destruction, and many enter through it. But small is the gate and narrow the road that leads to life, and only a few find it." What you choose to believe about God does matter. In fact, it is the most important choice you will make in your life.

I think we can all agree that people who don't have a relationship with God are not able to understand the truth of His Word. I used to think that only pertained to those who don't believe, but God has taught me, throughout my journey, that it pertains to us all. For all of us, God's Word is like a scrambled message that is hidden from us. *If we do not read or study God's Word daily, how will we ever truly understand His message to us or even truly know Him?*

Joshua 1:8 states, "This Book of the Law shall not depart from your mouth, but you shall meditate in it day and night, that you may observe to do according to all that is written in it. For then, you will make your way prosperous, and then you will have good success."

The two highlighted words in the above passage are simple, but they possess strong and different meanings. I looked up the definitions of these words in Webster's 1828 Dictionary.

Meditate: to dwell on anything in thought; to contemplate; to study.

Do: to apply or to perform.

So, in other words, we are to study the Word day and night so that, as we observe it, we can apply or perform it.

We, humans, are guilty of hitting the snooze button and turning over. Of course, everyone takes shortcuts in life, but ask yourself this: *Do we ever take the time to internally examine ourselves, filter through our behaviors, and identify our areas of laziness?* In the past, my answer to that question was no, but recently, while stuck on a plane for fifteen hours, I did just that and came to the conclusion that I had been lazy toward God. We all have at some point. That self-examination made me realize that I can do and understand better when it comes to my relationship with God.

So, we have to ask ourselves, are we cheating ourselves out of God's best for us by taking the easy route? I honestly don't know the answer to this, but we all know who does.

I remember reading this at some point last year, and it struck me then. "As a door turns on its hinges, so does the lazy man on his bed" (Proverbs 26:14, NKJV).

I needn't be this way; none of us do. We need to pursue God to the fullest. But what does it mean to pursue something? Webster's 1828 Dictionary tells us it means "to seek" or "to follow." So, to tie this all together, we are to seek, study, and apply God's Word in our daily lives. That is the only way we will understand everything that God wants and needs us to understand.

~Amen.

Today, reflect on where God is directing you. Reflect on your desire to know Him more so that you can understand His Word and grow closer to Him.

Day Twelve: Steps

Before I explain what God taught me through this photo, I would like to share how this photo came to be. It was taken in 2016 at Herd Base just off the Purari River in Papua New Guinea. I was about to board a ship that would take me to the Purari International Airport, at least that's what we called it. The Purari International Airport is just a small airstrip. Anyway, it was my last day in the country. I was heading home. I saw the sun just peeking over the ridgeline, and the thought, *Take your sunglasses and focus your camera through the lens on the sun*, came to me. I did just that.

I studied the resulting photo during the plane ride to Cairns, Australia, and felt that God was trying to teach me something. I started writing in my notes, and what I learned was pretty amazing.

In 2016, many things were going on in my life, and this photo was a metaphor for just that. God was teaching me how to see things through His perspective, not my own. I was viewing through a different lens. God's perspective at that time in my life was a bit blurry around the edges, but as I got closer to what He wanted me to see, it became much clearer.

Life is not always about being fast. It's about knowing your route and where you're headed. You may be in a position where you have already heard from God. Perhaps, He has told you His specific will for your life. Now, you are in the middle of the journey, and it is taking longer than planned. Opposition has a way of causing us to lose focus on what God promised us.

There are times when God steps in and changes your direction. When you find yourself in a vulnerable position, there are two very distinct attitudes you can choose to adopt. The first is always, "Poor me!" The second is trusting that God can turn any situation into good.

Faith is trusting that God has a purpose for every lesson He teaches you. Just remember, the direction He leads you may not take you along the path you want, but He knows best and will lead you through the obstacles (read Proverbs 14:15, 20:24).

God doesn't want us to be fearful of opposition. We need to understand God gets the greatest glory in your life in the face of your greatest resistance. The place where you were wounded the most is where God wants to show His greatest healing. The place where you have felt the weakest is where God wants to show His greatest strength. The place where you have felt most isolated and alone is where God wants to show you how close He is to you.

~Amen.

Today, reflect on the steps that God has placed before you and be encouraged. Even if things look hazy and your vision seems clouded, take baby steps forward. You aren't taking them by yourself. God is with you every step of the way.

Day Thirteen: Garbage In and Garbage Out

Even though I haven't been back to Papua New Guinea in three years, I still remember trash burning day. It happened every Thursday, and it produced, by far, the worst smell I have ever encountered. If someone were to ask me what I don't miss, my answer would be the smell of trash burning day. However, believe it or not, trash burning day taught me something. Does the phrase "garbage in and garbage out" have relevance in your life? Have you ever heard that phrase? While it certainly doesn't sound pleasant, the good news is that there is a positive spin on this saying that rings true. If we want good things out of life, we must put good things in.

Many of us treat life as though it is a magic hat that we can reach into and pull out whatever we need, whenever we need it. We make a habit of living hurried lives, but when a situation requires patience, we hope we can reach into our magic hat and produce that character trait at will. We also believe that we can over-commit our schedules, leaving very little time for our families. Then, when cracks begin to appear in our relationships, we think we will magically be able to connect with our family on a deeper level. The truth is, life doesn't work that way.

To get good things out of our lives, we must first put good things in them. If we want good health, we first choose healthy behaviors. If we want a successful marriage, we need to first instill in our relationship qualities to help it succeed. Succeeding at making changes like these requires our openness to God's truth and a willingness to receive the counsel, support, and encouragement of those who matter most to us.

In the end, however, we have to be intentional about acting on these influences and persevering in behavior and choices that are in harmony with God's Word. After all, we don't have a magic hat that allows us to pull something out of nothing.

~Amen.

Today, reflect on the negative behaviors in your life and decide to start bringing goodness into it. Remember, the positive character traits we seek can only result from a daily commitment to prioritize actions and decisions that please the Lord.

Day Fourteen: Motivation

I like to run, I always have. One day while in Kiunga, Papua New Guinea, I decided to go for a run. I did not know how far I would run; I just felt the push to run. I will let you in on a secret; when the Holy Spirit pushes or pulls you towards something, even if it's something as insignificant as going for a run, you should do it. God always taught me something during my runs in Kiunga.

On this particular day, after running two miles, I reached a turnaround point and began to feel demotivated. Have you ever felt that way about life? About your job? Have you ever started something that you didn't feel like finishing? I know I have. Sometimes, we have days that drag us down. I occasionally experience those kinds of days when I'm overseas, away from my family.

After I'd passed the turnaround point of my run and was on my way back, I was dragging, and I wanted to stop. Then, something interesting happened. One child fell into step with me and joined me. Then five more joined me. This went on until a total of thirteen kids were running along with me. They gave me the motivation to keep going and finish what I had started.

Here is what you can take away from this story: If you keep your mind on God and *do all things unto and for God* (read Colossians 3:23), He will put tools and individuals in your path to help you push through the most difficult parts and finish what you started. You just have to listen and keep your eyes open so that you don't miss it.

~Amen.

Today, reflect on what is demotivating you and lay it at God's feet. He will direct you and bring things and people into your life that will motivate you; focus on those things or people.

Day Fifteen: Contentment

How many of us can say, "I am not jealous of anyone else or envious of what others have. If God gave it to them, then I want them to enjoy it."

The Word says, "Let your conduct be without covetousness; be content with such things as you have" (Hebrews 13:5, NKJV). I believe God tests us to see if we will live by this verse.

There are times when He puts someone in front of us who has exactly what we want, just to see how we respond. Until we can pass His "I am happy for you because you are blessed" test, we will not be given more than what we have at present.

If you have asked God for something and He hasn't given it to you, rest assured that He is not holding out on you. He simply wants to make sure that you rid yourself of jealousy and make Him your top priority. God wants us to prosper in every way. He wants people to see His goodness and how well He takes care of us, but we must desire God more than we desire His blessings.

Let's dig a bit deeper. Have you ever really wondered or even asked yourself what being content means? Without having experienced this and having seen it firsthand, I would not be able to speak of this, nor would I be where I am today. True contentment is a heart attitude. No one is happier than a truly thankful person, a truly content person.

By visiting different countries and having seen this firsthand, I've learned that being content means *being satisfied to the point where nothing disturbs you no matter what's going on, but not satisfied to the point that you never want anything to change.*

Every time I get on the plane to head home, whether it's leaving Papua New Guinea or Afghanistan, I cannot help but reflect on certain truths in my life.

The people we surround ourselves with will raise or lower our standards. They help us become the best version of ourselves or encourage us to become a lesser version of ourselves. We become who we hang around. No man becomes great on his own. No woman becomes great on her own. The people that God brings into our lives and puts around us help us become greater. We all need people in our lives who raise our standards, remind us of our essential purpose and challenge us to become the best version of ourselves.

> I know what it is to be in need, and I know what it is to have plenty. I have learned the secret of being content in any and every situation, whether well fed or hungry, whether living in plenty or in want…And my God will meet all your needs according to the riches of His glory in Christ Jesus.
>
> Philippians 4:12, 19 (NIV)

In Philippians 4:10–19, the apostle Paul seems to take a supply-side view of spirituality. He seems less focused on his needs and those of the church though they're great, and more focused on God's supply because it is greater. Do you see your needs through your supply, or are you always missing your supply because all you see are your needs? That is faith's greatest question.

God's greatest goal isn't to get us to a place where we don't have any needs. Without an awareness of our needs, we would begin to think we didn't need Him. God is inviting us to live from the supply side. Here, we spend more time acknowledging and accessing His supply than we do stressing about our needs. The very need you are asking God to eliminate in your life might be the space He created to show His supply. Embrace it. Once you choose to view your needs from the supply side, you will find yourself like Paul in Philippians 4:12; content whatever the circumstances.

~Amen.

Today, ask God to show you the areas of your life where you have given into jealousy and ask Him to help you rearrange your priorities.

Day Sixteen: Trials

We all know what is required of us when we want to make physical improvements to our bodies, especially if our goal is to gain muscle. It requires putting our bodies through some serious trials in the weight room. During those trials and workouts, we break down our muscle fibers. They don't grow during the breakdown process, but they do during the restoration and buildup process that follows. During the restoration process, we consume protein, drink water, take amino acids, rest, and eat healthily.

The spiritual process works the same way. In order for there to be a restoration process that enables spiritual growth, there must first be a trial or breakdown process from which we need to be restored. So, what does the restoration process look like after we have gone through trials and our spiritual muscle has broken down, and we feel utterly defeated?

The restoration process brings with it a series of choices. We choose to worship instead of worry. We choose to pray instead of panic. We choose to operate in faith instead of fear. When our world is crashing down around us, we stop and talk to the One who created the world. It states in 2 Corinthians 12:9 (NKJV), "My grace is sufficient for you, for My strength is made perfect in weakness. Therefore most gladly I will rather boast in my infirmities, that the power of Christ may rest upon me."

I am sure you have heard many times that *God uses our trials for His good.* As cliche as that sounds, it is very true. God uses our trials to reveal our spiritual condition and our spiritual character. When we decide to improve our physical selves, our true character shows when we find all sorts of excuses not to exercise.

Can we really know the truth about someone's spiritual condition when everything is going well? No, we can't. The reason we can't is that, often, a person's true nature doesn't reveal itself when they appear happy and fulfilled and everything looks good on the surface. It's the same at the gym. We go in, we start slow, and choose the easy workouts until we get a trainer who brings the pain. No pain, no gain.

It doesn't take long after things begin to go wrong that the real state of our spiritual condition begins to surface. The worse things get, the more our spiritual character is bared. When we strip away the blessings, the successes, the prosperity, and the health, we find out what we are really made of and where we are spiritually.

You may think I'm crazy for saying this, but I'm thankful for the trials in my life, and I'm a strong believer because I've been drawn toward God during those trials. Through trials, we are forced into the presence of God, and that is the best place we can possibly be.

Take note that good times do not do this. The more severe the trial, the more likely it is that our prayer life will improve. However, we need to draw closer to Him even when everything is great.

God also uses our trials to humble us. How? Well, Spurgeon once said, "You have two choices. You can either be humble or humbled."

Trouble is humbling. Job experienced this. To summarize, Job spent half of his life building this fortune, and then the Lord just wiped it out and killed everyone in his family but his wife and then humbled him. I believe God did that to make a point.

The point He made was that His servant would be humbled and never lose faith. Despite everything he suffered, Job didn't curse God. In fact, Job said in his humility, in Job 42:6, "Therefore I despise myself and repent in dust and ashes." Job was repenting in a pile of ash. *Could it be that this is where God wants us to be?* Job had no trust in the flesh and no confidence in himself. He was helpless and hopeless and was clinging to the mercy, grace, and power of God. When Job was at the end of his endurance, God opened the floodgates, and more blessings than he ever thought possible were poured down on him.

God also uses our trials to draw us closer to Him. First Corinthians 10:13 (NKJV) says, "No temptation has overtaken you except such as is common to man; but God is faithful, who will not allow you to be tempted beyond what you are able, but with temptation will also make the way of escape, that you may be able to bear it."

We will experience trials in our lives that we can't endure alone, but God will give us the grace to endure them so that while we are enduring them, we experience the great grace of the Lord. Joshua 1:9 states, "Have I not commanded you? Be strong and of good courage; do not be afraid, nor be dismayed, for the Lord your God is with you wherever you go."

God also uses our trials to perfect His strength. Two Corinthians 12:9 states that "strength is made perfect in weakness."

The 1828 Webster's Dictionary defines strength as "power or vigor of any kind. Power of resisting attacks." According to this definition, we are not only to endure trials so that God can display His grace but also because God wants us to be powerful. God wants to use us to change the world as He did with Paul.

"But God has chosen the foolish things of the world to put to shame the wise, and God has chosen the weak things of the world to put to shame the things which are mighty" (1 Corinthians 1:27, NKJV).

~Amen

Today, reflect on the trials in your life and look at them as if they are spiritual workouts. The truth is that you will experience difficulty during the workout, and your endurance will be tested, but once you make it through, you will be so glad that you stuck it out. Take heart in this: there will be a day where you will be able to look back at your path and say, I'm glad this happened.

Day Seventeen: Reproduction

Have you ever wondered how the law of reproduction works? If a farmer goes out with a trailer load of beans and plants them in a barren field, what fruit does he expect the plants to bear? Watermelon? Cucumbers? No, of course not. The seeds he plants are going to produce beans. He doesn't doubt it. He doesn't question it because he knows that he will reap what he sows. That is the law of reproduction, and it applies to every single area of your life.

The Bible says in 2 Corinthians 9:6–7, "Remember this: Whoever sows sparingly will also reap sparingly, and whoever sows generously will also reap generously. Each of you should give what you have decided in your heart to give, not reluctantly or under compulsion, for God loves a cheerful giver."

That can work in your life positively or negatively. If you are planting seeds of kindness, you know what? People are going to be kind to you. If you forgive others, they are going to be forgiving of you. If you're generous, people are going to be generous to you. However, if you are angry all of the time, people are going to respond in anger. If you cheat other people, people are going to cheat you. If you gossip about other people, guess what? People are going to gossip about you.

The law of reproduction states, you reap what you sow, but the principle of multiplication states you will always reap more than you sow.

When you put one kernel of corn in the ground, you don't get one kernel of corn back. You get a cornstalk with multiple ears on it and hundreds of kernels on each of those ears. That is the exponential power that God has established the universe to handle. You always get more out of it than you put into it.

This is why we should never, ever attack our attackers. Why? Because we don't want to get caught up in the chain. No matter what anyone says to us, we shouldn't say anything bad in return because if we do, we will reap more than we sowed. What we should choose to do is the exact opposite. We want to bless them. We want to pray for them. Why? Because that's what we want to receive, and we always reap more than we sow.

"One person gives freely, yet gains even more; another withholds unduly, but comes to poverty" (Proverbs 11:24, NIV).

~Amen.

Today, reflect on the law reproduction. Reflect on how you are treating others and how you want to be treated.

Day Eighteen: Pray More than Once

The one question everyone has is, *Why doesn't God answer every prayer we pray?* I struggled with this for a long time and still do at times. I believe we are more at fault than we want to admit. How so? We all tend to get frustrated and stop praying because our prayer isn't answered when we think it should be.

Let's face it; if God answered every prayer we prayed, we would never learn to lean on Him. I know that I would be praying everywhere I go, and the next thing I know, I'd be walking into a light pole. God doesn't answer every prayer the moment we want Him to because He wants us to learn to lean on Him and appreciate the blessings that He has bestowed on us.

Maybe you're the type of person who feels that asking once is enough, and when nothing happens, you believe that your answer to that prayer is *no*. I agree with that to a point. I used to think that way, too, before I started to learn more and more about God's Word.

Jesus says, "Ask, and it will be given to you; seek, and you will find, knock and it will be opened to you" (Matthew 7:7, NKJV).

Let's look at this from a different perspective. Parents don't like it when their children ask for something over and over again when they've already been told no. It is understandable, therefore, to think God would feel this way as well. After all, no one wants to sound ungrateful. The truth, however, is the opposite. God does not see repeated prayers as nagging or begging.

"Then Jesus told his disciples a parable to show them that they should always pray and not give up...And will not God bring about justice for His chosen ones, who cry out to Him day and night? Will he keep putting them off?" (Luke 18:1, 7, NIV)

In this parable, a widow pestered a judge for justice until he relented. Instead of criticizing the woman for being such a pest, Jesus held her up as a hero and invited all believers to be just like her.

Now that we know God is inviting us to be like the woman in the book of Luke, let's cover the three levels of prayer.

Ask, Seek, and Knock

I believe if we know His will, we are to *ask*. If we do not know His will, we are to *seek*. If we know His will but the answer has not come, we are to *knock* until the door opens.

Level One

"Ask, and it will be given to you."

When we ask, we have the promise from God that we will receive it. When we know God's will in a matter, we can ask and have the confidence that we will receive it.

Level Two

"…seek, and you will find…"

We are to keep seeking with an intensity that goes beyond simply presenting our issues, and He promises that we will find His perfect will for our lives as long as we don't give up.

Level Three

"…know, and it will be opened to you…"

The first two levels lead to this. We keep asking, seeking, and knocking. When we keep knocking and never give up, we hold to God's promise that "it will be opened to you."

Believe it or not, God deals with us as we do our children. Wait, what!? Think about it, when our children are young, we teach them to *ask* for things. As they grow older, we teach them to *seek* answers. When they are young adults, hopefully, they have learned how to *knock*.

God will answer our prayers in different ways. Those ways are as follows:

The answer could be *direct* at times, which means that when we pray, we will almost immediately see or hear the answer.

The answer could also be *denied* at times, which means that God is reassuring us that He knows what is best for us.

The answer could also be *delayed*. Sometimes, God puts us in a holding pattern; the answer will eventually come but in His time. This stretches our faith in Him.

The answer could be *different* from what we expect. However, just because He answers our prayers in a different way does not mean that He didn't answer them.

We all know that praying is simply talking to God. We all know that He loves us and wants the best for us. We are all searching for two things: God and answers. Wouldn't you agree?

Psalm 42:1–2 (NKJV) says, "As the deer pants for streams of water, so my soul pants for You, O God. My soul thirsts for God, for the living God."

We can go to God in prayer and find Him and get answers, just as the deer finds water in a stream when it is thirsty. Just remember, God speaks to us through His Word, and we speak to God through our prayers and praises.

~Amen.

Today, reflect on listening to God's voice closely so that the pathway you follow is clear and is God's alone.

Day Nineteen: Physics

This wouldn't be a book about seeing God in everyday life if it didn't include a physics lesson. What does physics have to do with everyday life? Follow me while we glide into this concept.

This concept, illustrated by the physics of an aircraft, came to me while I was flying over Afghanistan in the helicopter I maintain.

There are four forces that act on an aircraft.

Lift is the force that acts at a right angle to the direction of motion through the air. Lift is created by differences in air pressure.

Weight is the force of gravity that acts in a downward direction.

Thrust is the force that propels a flying machine in the direction of motion.

Drag is the force that acts opposite to the direction of motion. Drag is caused by friction and differences in air pressure.

God has taught me that all four of these forces represent the people and struggles that have come in and out of our lives.

There are those who put a spring in other people's steps. They essentially lift others' spirits even when the weight seems to be too much. I call these people *lifters*.

Some make others feel like the weight of the world is on their shoulders after being around them. I call these people the *weighers*. They weigh your life down.

Some want to help us succeed and do better in life, despite the obstacles. I call these people *thrusters*. They thrust us into success.

Some always look at the negative side of things and are always looking for sympathy. These people drag themselves, and those around them, through life. I call these people *drags*. They drag us down in life.

We have a choice to go through life as a *lifter,* a *weigher,* a *thruster,* or a *drag.* We have the choice to allow those around us to lift us up, thrust us forward, weigh us down, or drag us through our daily lives.

However, just as the aircraft needs all of these forces to fly, God allows all types of people to walk in and out of our lives to keep us balanced. Confused? Let's dive a little deeper.

When an airplane is flying straight and level at a constant speed, the *lift* it produces balances its *weight.* The *thrust* the airplane produces balances its *drag.* However, these balances of forces change as the airplane rises and descends, just as we do in life. When we start *lifting,* the *weight* tends to pile on a lot stronger, and when we are *thrust* into something in our lives, the *drag* of life tends to pile up as well.

What we need to understand about all of this is that God wants us to balance our lives in order to become what He is trying to mold us into. We must allow our lives to have some *lift, weight, thrust,* and *drag.*

~Amen.

Today, reflect on yourself. Are you lifting people up or thrusting them forward? Or are you weighing people down and dragging them through your daily life struggles?

Day Twenty: Control

Have you ever reached a place in your life where things were out of your control? A place where you were spiritually drowning, dealing with depression, dealing with addictions, financial upset, relationship dramas? The list goes on and on. What you are about to read can and will make a difference in your life if you choose to apply it.

When a situation reaches the point where you want to throw your hands up and say, "It's out of my hands," that's normally a sign of desperation and defeat. I want to share a new perspective with you today.

Most of us overestimate how much control we have and underestimate how many choices we have. The complete truth is that we never really have control, but we do have a choice. Instead of seeing your lack of control as a problem, start seeing it as an opportunity to rely more on God.

At any given moment, you have the power to say, "This is not how the story ends."

Remember, just because it's no longer in your hands doesn't mean that it's not in God's. When the situation is out of your hands, it's the perfect time to put it in His. Unlike your hands, God's are never lacking or limited.

As God's Word states, "Wealth and honor come from you; you are the ruler of all things. In your hands are strength and power to exalt and give strength to all" (1 Chronicles 29:12, NIV).

Life may not look the way you want it to right now, but instead of placing a lid on your expectations and relying only on the supply that you can provide, place yourself under the mighty hand of God, where unlimited power and strength reside.

~Amen.

Today, reflect on the choice to give God control. He will take that spiritual drowning and use it as an uplifting and overflowing wave that will connect to those with whom you come in contact. He will take control of the depression and addictions of life that control your life and suppress them.

Day Twenty-One: Dash

Watching my dad struggle with cancer really opened my eyes to many understandings about life, and I will forever cherish the conversations we had during that time.

My dad taught me the four L's of life:
- Listen to those who came before.
- Learn from those who have walked before you.
- Laugh with those around you.
- Love those around you.

Through my walk with Jesus, I have learned there is a struggle within that we each deal with when death arrives. I learned that to cope with death, we are to lean on Jesus and those around us. We have to take it breath by breath and day by day, and it will get better and better.

Have you ever heard the phrase, "They were too young; that's too bad." My question is, what does age have to do with death? I have asked myself this very question. We all have something in common when it comes to our tombstones. Each of us will have two kinds of numbers visible for everyone to see who comes to visit. They are the birth date, which is the day that we began this beautiful, blurry, chaotic journey we call life, and our death date, which is the day we passed on to do bigger and greater things with and for God. However, there is one small detail that we also all have in common that gets overlooked. That small detail is the "dash" between the two dates.

What does this important symbol mean? The "dash" on all our tombstones will reflect how long a life we lived and the kind of life we have lived. Some will strive to fill their years with meaning and purpose. Others will just live a really long time. Don't mis-understand me; the desire to live a long life is something we all should understand, but none of us is guaranteed tomorrow. We only have today. So, it is important to fill this moment, and every moment after this, with things that matter. When all is said and done, it boils down to faith in Christ, a strong relationship with your family, and pouring your life into others.

Evan Esar, an American humorist, once said, "You can't do anything about the length of your life, but you can do something about its width and depth."

~Amen.

Today, reflect on your "dash." What will it symbolize about the years you were given? What kind of footprint do you want to leave on this world?

Printed in the USA
CPSIA information can be obtained
at www.ICGtesting.com
LVHW020011151123
763986LV00077B/2274